C000243762

NORWICH CITY

A Portrait in Old Picture Postcards

by

Dick Middleton and Paul Standley

Foreword
by
Dave Stringer

S. B. Publications

CONTENTS

CONTENTS

CONTENTS

Front Cover: Norwich City F.C. 1959/60 after having been promoted to Division Two.
Team (back row): B. Thurlow, T. Allcock, R. McCrohan, S. Kennon, B. Butler, T. Bly, M. Crowe, H. Topping
(front row): E. Crossan, J. Hill, B. Whitehouse, R. Ashman, B. Larkin, R. Brennan, B. Punton.

Back Cover: Cigarette card cartoon caricature, 1933;
W. Bushell, Norwich City 1909/10, Gallaher's cigarette card.

FOREWORD

This book depicts the life of Norwich City Football Club in a unique way.

Dick Middleton and Paul Standley have put together a fascinating and rare collection of postcards which illustrates the rise of the club between 1902/03 and 1992/93. A span of 90 years, in which time there have been several ups and downs. I have been privileged to have been involved in thirty of these years which arguably have been the most successful the club has known.

Although this success has come in recent years, to reach this stage so many people in numerous ways have contributed to lay the foundations on which the present-day successes have been achieved. Without a history there is no present, and this book, 'Norwich City – A Portrait In Old Picture Postcards' is, I feel, a tribute to every player, official and member of staff who has worked so hard to further the well being of Norwich City Football Club.

Dave Stringer,
Former Manager,
Norwich City F. C.

INTRODUCTION

The first postcards were issued in Europe in 1869, and one year later appeared in Britain. These early cards were smaller than those we know today and bore no illustrations. The address was written on one side and the message on the other. In the 1890s the first picture postcards were published. The illustration and message were obliged to share one side of the card and naturally there was little room left for a message of reasonable length. In 1902 the Post Office issued new regulations for postcards: the message and address to be on one side and the illustration on the reverse. The postcard as we know it today had been born.

Sending and collecting postcards soon became very popular and a national craze. Postage was cheap ($\frac{1}{2}$ d), delivery fast (morning and afternoon deliveries were the norm) and telephones rare. In the early years of this century up to the first world war, 500 million postcards were sent annually.

Each family would have their own postcard album with cards posted from friends and relatives from around the country and abroad. By 1920 however, the 'Golden Age of Postcards' had declined dramatically. Postage increased and telephones gradually replaced the quick message previously sent on a postcard. This resulted in the once cherished postcard album to be put in the attic, to gather dust for the next fifty years.

At the height of this postcard boom, the publishers of these picture postcards had not only provided a cheap source of correspondence, but more importantly had provided an invaluable source of social history and an insight into everyday life in those bygone days. Not only a typical beach scene, but local events, disasters, transport and ordinary street scenes.

Over the last twenty years people have rediscovered these gems of the past in their attics. Gradually, postcard collecting was reborn and now there are numerous collectors of old picture postcards of every possible subject, including football.

Norwich City's formation coincided with the beginning of the 'Golden Age' and the fledgling years of the 'Canaries' are particularly well documented in this form. Local publishers such as Wilkinson's, Haywood T. Kidd and Swain's must have invested many hours capturing the early characters and events involving the 'Canaries'. Although there have been no league championships to celebrate and cup-fighting heroics have never led to an F.A. Cup final appearance, Norwich City Football Club has had its fair share of ups and downs, many of which have been recorded on postcards; the majority in this book reproduced for the first time. The reader may wonder why there are so few post-war postcards included in the book. The simple answer is that very few were published and to the authors' knowledge are rare.

NORWICH CITY — A SHORT HISTORY

For several years the leading soccer club in Norwich had been the Church of England side, C.E.Y.M.S., so when two of its former members, schoolmasters Bob Webster and Joe Nutchey, called a public meeting on 17th June, 1902 to propose the formation of a rival Norwich City club, a few eyebrows were raised. Following a lively yet amicable debate between those for and against, however, the motion to proceed was carried and the new club was launched. Webster was elected the chairman with Nutchey the treasurer, and the club joined the Norfolk & Suffolk League. Blue and white halved shirts with white knickers were chosen as team colours and the council-owned Newmarket Road ground was leased for home games.

In their first season City finished third in the league and lost their first ever F.A. Cup-tie 0–5 to Lowestoft. In 1903/04 they reached the semi-finals of the Southern Division of the F.A. Amateur Cup, but part way through 1904/05 the F.A. demanded to see the club's books and reported irregularities over certain payments to players. The payments were considered to be in violation of amateur rules and City were instantly expelled from the F.A. Amateur Cup. A series of urgent meetings followed and at length the club declared itself professional. A limited company was formed, John Bowman from Queen's Park Rangers was appointed manager/secretary and the club was elected to the Southern League. They were, however, permitted to complete their Norfolk & Suffolk League programme provided they did not field any of the professional players being recruited. They finished as champions of the League.

The club remained at Newmarket Road until the end of 1907/08 when, in order to present an image more befitting their new professional status, they moved to new premises — 'The Nest', a quaint little ground built on the site of filled-in chalk workings in Rosary Road. The previous season club colours were changed to yellow and green and it was around this time Norwich City's link with the famous Norwich breed of canary came into being. From then until the outbreak of World War One the team stayed in the lower reaches of the table, conceding ten goals at Swindon in September 1908, and had only F.A. Cup successes, notably against holders Sheffield Wednesday, Liverpool, Sunderland and Tottenham Hotspur to look back on.

Competition ceased during the war but the club kept going with a series of friendlies mostly against locally-based military units but by December 1917 the club had incurred heavy debts and the receiver was called in. In February 1919, however, a new company was formed, Major Frank Buckley was appointed manager and the club prepared for season 1919/20 still in the Southern League.

In 1920/21 they became founder members of the Football League's new third division but did not get into the top half until 1929/30 when they finished eighth and crushed Coventry 10–2 in the process. An otherwise lean decade is probably remembered for two inglorious cup defeats by Luton and Corinthians. Matters worsened in 1930/31 when they finished bottom and had to seek re-election but they recovered well, were third in 1932/33 and gained their first promotion in 1933/34, winning the Division Three (South) championship in style.

City's second division debut resulted in a 1–2 reverse at Brentford — Ken Burditt scoring their goal — and their first win came two days later at home to Bury. When the season ended with City in fourteenth place, the F.A. declared 'The Nest' unsuitable for larger crowds. The board were strung into frantic action culminating in the move to Carrow Road, the club's present home. For the next four seasons the team comfortably held their own in the higher grade but just when they seemed set to launch a challenge they were relegated. They failed to make any impact during 1938/39 and arrived at the last game of the season needing to beat fellow strugglers Nottingham Forest 4–0 to stay up and send Forest down. As it happened City managed only a 1–0 win so Forest survived at City's expense by 0.048 of a goal.

After three matches of the 1939/40 season, war again brought proceedings to a temporary halt and between then and 1941/42 City took part in regionalised war league and cup competitions but when travel restrictions were imposed the 'Canaries' found themselves out on a geographical limb with local friendlies now their only source of action. In a South Regional League match on Christmas Day 1940 City trounced a make-shift Brighton side 18–0 to register the club's all-time record win. Six of the goals came from Ipswich Town's centre-forward Fred Chadwick, one of many 'guests' who assisted the club during these dark days.

The post-war era began with City back in Division Three (South) and they finished the first two seasons second from bottom, being re-elected on both occasions. They then hit a purple patch finishing in the top seven five seasons out of six, narrowly missing promotion in 1950/51, and scoring a club record ninety-nine league goals plus winning 8−1 at Shrewsbury in 1952/53. There were also memorable cup wins against Liverpool and at Highbury and a home defeat by Portsmouth in front of 43,129 spectators. In 1956/57 the tide dramatically turned as City slumped to the bottom and had to apply for re-election for their fourth and final time. They went a record twenty-six games without a win and were knocked out of the cup by non-league Bedford Town. To add to the miseries more heavy debts plunged the club into dire financial straits and it needed a public appeal for funds and a new board of directors to stave off the disaster of folding. The change did the trick and by finishing eighth in 1957/58 City 'made the cut' when the top and bottom halves of the Third Division's north and south sections formed the new Divisions Three and Four. The real story of 1958/59 is always the team's magnificent march to the F.A. Cup semi-finals, coming within a whisker of being the first Third Division side to reach the final but they finished fourth in the table too and went two places better in 1959/60, gaining promotion as runners-up to Southampton.

Back in Division Two for their second spell City started well, finishing fourth in 1960/61, their highest placing of the sixties. The Football League Cup was inaugurated that season and in 1961/62 City became the second winners of the trophy, beating Rochdale over a two-legged final. There was no Wembley appearance or European place as bait in those days, so several leading clubs boycotted the competition. Even so there were enough good teams taking part to make City's victory a fine achievement. Their record League Cup win came in November 1963 with a 7−1 victory at Halifax. In 1962/63 Terry Allcock scored a record thirty-seven league and cup goals and the team reached round six of the F.A. Cup before losing at home to Leicester in front of the ground record 43,984 crowd. Their best cup performance of the sixties was unquestionably the 2−1 victory at Old Trafford in February 1967.

The seventies started quietly but as 1971/72 got under way City charged to the top of the table and by 29th May 1972 had clinched the Second Division title and, for the first time, a place in the First Division. Their opening gambit in Division One was a 1−1 home draw against Everton (Jim Bone scoring) and their first win was at neighbouring Ipswich three days later when they beat Town 2−1. Initially City's direct style of play paid dividends but once the opposition 'worked them out' they began to struggle and only avoided immediate relegation in the final match of the season.

Over the next thirteen seasons City went between divisions one and two, going down in 1973/74, 1980/81 and 1984/85 but bouncing back up at the first attempt on all three occasions. They set a Football League record in 1978/79 by drawing twenty-three of their forty-two matches and on the transfer front, in March 1980, Kevin Reeves was sold for £1,000,000 to become the first of seven City players to reportedly have commanded a seven figure fee. Over the same period City made three Wembley appearances reaching the League Cup finals of 1972/73 and 1974/75, losing in turn to Tottenham Hotspur and Aston Villa, and the Milk Cup final of 1984/85 beating Sunderland. Unfortunately that triumph was tempered by relegation soon after.

1988/89 not only saw City finish fourth in Division One, their best season ever, but also reach the semi-finals of the F.A. Cup only to lose 0−1 to Everton after crushing little Sutton United 8−0 along the way. The result was repeated at Hillsborough in 1991/92 when, devastatingly, second division Sunderland shattered City's Wembley hopes and avenged their 1984/85 Milk Cup defeat. At the time of going to print the 'Canaries' are proudly 'perched' on top of the F.A.'s new Premier Division. Perhaps 1992/93 will be the year, now the ban on English clubs has been lifted, City will be able to take their place in Europe, something denied them on previous occasions through no fault of their own.

It is hoped this book will not only bring back happy memories for the more seasoned campaigners but will also make enjoyable reading for the younger enthusiast interested in the club's fascinating history. Either way it has been our privilege and pleasure to present it to you.

Dick Middleton, Caister-on-sea.

Paul Standley, Wymondham.

JAMES PRATT ADDISON SHIELDS, 1902/03

Jimmy had the distinction of scoring Norwich City's first ever goal — albeit in a friendly. On Saturday, 6th September 1902, Harwich & Parkeston provided the opposition for City's inaugural match. In front of 2,000 spectators at Newmarket Road, Harwich went ahead just before half-time but with some fifteen minutes remaining, inside-left Shields fastened onto left winger Tommy Newell's cross to equalise and earn his team a 1–1 draw. Jimmy's playing days were cut short by injury and he made only four other appearances, scoring four times. For several years he and his wife ran a tobacconist and cigar merchant shop in Magdalen Street, Norwich but later on he moved to Ipswich and became a park attendant. He died in 1947.

NORWICH CITY FOOTBALL CLUB, 1903/04

This card is the only one, to the authors' knowledge, depicting a team group from the club's amateur days. The players, from left to right are: *(back)* F. Rackham, W. Cooks, R. Pointer, H. Sayer; *(middle)* E. Chamberlain, P. Gooch, R. Collinson (Capt), T. Newell, E. Harris; *(front)* H. King, J. Cutmore. This season City forfeited their place in the English Cup after drawing with West Norwood in the 3rd qualifying round. The replay clashed with an F.A. Amateur Cup tie against Harwich & Parkeston and participation in that competition was preferred. After five successful rounds they eventually lost at home to Ealing. Domestically they won the Norfolk & Norwich Hospital Cup in its inaugural year and the Norfolk Charity Cup (both displayed above) and finished third in the Norfolk & Suffolk League.

Back row: left to right, Archer, McEwen (Captain), Bushell, Warnes, *2nd Row:* Miles (Trainer),
J. W. Bowman (Manager), Childs, Cummings, Williams, Rose, Bemment, McQueen (Assistant Trainer),
3rd Row: Muir, Graham, Wilkinson, Ronaldson, Ross, Brindley, Linward,
Front Row: Vigar, Livingstone.

NORWICH CITY F.C., 1905/06

In this their first season after turning professional, City finished 7th (which was to prove their best ever) in the Southern League and reached the second round of the English Cup before going out 0−3 away to Manchester United. That season the 'Citizens', as they were then known, had their first taste of continental opposition when Club Athletique Professionel Parisien visited Newmarket Road for a friendly on 28th September 1905. City won 11−0 with six of the goals coming from Davie Ross, later to be transferred to Manchester City for £650 − a then Southern League record.

NEWMARKET ROAD, c. 1905

James 'Punch' McEwen leads out the City team ready to do battle. The player with a bandaged boot is his full-back partner Arthur Archer whilst the goalkeeper, wearing cap, is thought to be Charlie Williams (ex-Woolwich Arsenal and Manchester City). McEwen, a member of the Bury team that hammered Derby County 6—0 in the 1902/03 Cup Final, skippered City for two seasons before being appointed player/manager for 1907/08. Early in 1909 though he left for Highbury where he served for many years as coach, trainer and kit man. He died in Barnes in May 1942. In the right background, the wooden pavilion survives today virtually as it was, except the splendid white paint has long since disappeared.

GRAND SAVE BY KITCHEN

City v. West Ham

NORWICH CITY v. WEST HAM UNITED, 1905

George Kitchen, the West Ham goalkeeper, gets down low to halt a City attack during a match at Newmarket Road on 7th October 1905. City won 1−0, thanks to Duncan Ronaldson's first half goal, to register their first ever Southern League victory. In the return fixture at Upton Park on 10th February 1906, City were well and truly 'Hammered' 6−1 and Kitchen, West Ham's penalty taker at the time, scored his side's second goal from the spot. He later saved a penalty from City's Arthur Archer. Between 1905 and 1911 Kitchen made 184 appearances in the West Ham goal, scoring 5 penalties. Interestingly, he was also a golf professional.

NEWMARKET ROAD SPECTATORS, c. 1906

A typical crowd scene at Newmarket Road in the early days of this century — everyone sedately posed and not a bare head in sight. Note how several of the young boys in the foreground are leaning sideways towards the centre to ensure the camera catches them. For the record: the largest crowd for a Norwich City match at Newmarket Road was an estimated 11,500 (precise figures were rarely reported in those days) for the Southern League clash with Tottenham Hotspur on 14th April 1906; whilst the average attendance over their six seasons at the ground was around 5,200 per game.

NORWICH CITY F.C., 1907/08

This is the most common, and the most popular card from the period. The minature portraits make a welcome departure from the traditional team group. 1907/08 was City's last season at Newmarket Road and is probably best remembered for their first round English Cup k.o. of holders Sheffield Wednesday on 11th January 1908. Playing in conventional boots on an icy pitch, Wednesday were comfortably beaten 2−0 (Bauchop, Allsopp) by an inspired City team wearing 'Rubber soled shoes'. In round 2, City were drawn at home to Fulham but agreed to switch the tie to Craven Cottage for a guaranteed payment of £650, and lost 1−2.

'THE NEST' SITE, ROSARY ROAD, April 1908

'The Nest' was built on a filled-in chalk pit in Thorpe Hamlet in the area bounded by Rosary Road, St. Leonard's Road and Gas Hill. The pit was named 'Ruymp's Hole' after Robert Ruymp & Son, the brick and tile merchant who worked the site in the late 19th century, and it was close to Lollard's Pit, well known as a place for the burning of heretics in the middle ages. This view is looking east up towards St. Leonard's Road and shows the height and scale of the cliff which had to be 'retained' by a 50ft-high concrete wall.

'THE NEST' UNDER CONSTRUCTION, August 1908

The huge concrete retaining wall is shown here under construction. The card, dated August 1908, shows the state of progress just a month short of the planned opening! The ground appears roughly level, following the movement of an estimated 200,000 tons of chalk and earth but at this seemingly late stage the playing surface is yet to be laid and the covered accommodation for spectators (see page 15) yet to be erected.

THE NEST,
Norwich City Football Ground. Aug:08   Copyright

'THE NEST', LOOKING WEST, August 1908

Another early view of 'The Nest'; looking west towards Rosary Road and the city of Norwich beyond. This card, also dated August 1908, suggests plenty to be done before the start of the season. For instance, the five terraced houses immediately to the right of the gap (see centre), which the club had purchased, had yet to make way for a changing/bathing pavilion and offices. One of the house numbers, 51 Rosary Road, remained as the club's registered address.

PLAY UP! 'NORWICH CANARIES', c. 1908

Precisely when the club adopted the Norwich Canary as its emblem and nickname is not absolutely clear, although the change of team colours from the original blue and white to yellow and green for the season 1907/08, and followed by the naming of the new ground as 'The Nest', points to it being around that time. This attractive card is one of only a very few Norwich City postcards to be printed in colour. Most others were either black and white or sepia.

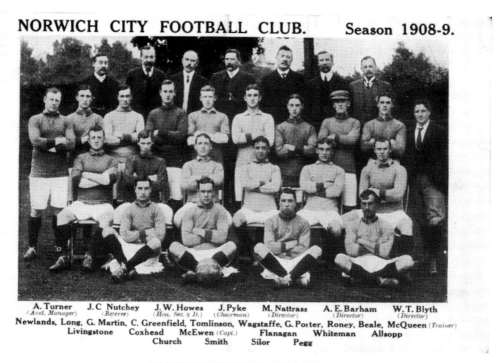

NORWICH CITY FOOTBALL CLUB. Season 1908-9.

A. Turner   J. C Nutchey   J. W. Howes   J. Pyke   M. Nattrass   A. E. Barham   W. T. Blyth
(Asst. Manager)   (Referee)   (Hon. Sec. & D.)   (Chairman)   (Director)   (Director)   (Director)

Newlands, Long, G. Martin, C. Greenfield, Tomlinson, Wagstaffe, G. Porter, Roney, Beale, McQueen (Trainer)

Livingstone   Coxhead   McEwen (Capt.)   Flanagan   Whiteman   Allsopp

Church   Smith   Silor   Pegg

NORWICH CITY F.C., 1908/09

In their first season at 'The Nest', City finished third from bottom in the Southern League and third from top in the midweek United League. 1908/09 brought the club's heaviest ever defeat – a 2–10 trouncing at Swindon. They were also humbled 1–7 at Reading but gained some revenge for that when, after two drawn games, they put the 'Biscuitmen' out of the English Cup (see page 14) to earn themselves a second round trip to Liverpool. There, against all odds, City silenced the 'Kop' by winning 3–2 with John Smith netting an injury-time winner. Disappointingly, the run ended in round 3 away to runners-up-to-be, Bristol City.

NORWICH CITY. V. FULHAM.

FIRST MATCH AT 'THE NEST', September 1908

The first public match at 'The Nest' took place on Tuesday, 1st September 1908 when Norwich City entertained second division Fulham in a friendly. In front of 3,300 spectators, City Chairman, Mr. John Pyke, kicked-off to formally open the new ground, then 2 goals from centre-forward John Smith sealed a 2−1 home win. In this picture Fulham are seen attacking the Norwich goal. The referee (second from right) is Joe Nutchey, one of the club's founders. Note the concrete retaining wall is far from complete but the single tier stand, transferred from Newmarket Road, is in place.

READING v. NORWICH CITY, January 1909

City were originally due to play their first round F.A. cup-tie at home but after opponents Reading objected to the size of the Rosary Road pitch, the F.A. switched the game to neutral Stamford Bridge. That match ended goal-less and the replay at Elm Park was also drawn. In the second replay, at Villa Park, it was 2−2 after 90 minutes and with a third replay looming, 'Little Jack' Flanagan popped up to end the saga 4 minutes from the end of extra time. The above action shot is from the 1−1 draw at Elm Park and gives the impression of the ball having just whistled past Peter Roney (in goalmouth), City's goalkeeper's right-hand post.

NORWICH CITY v. SOUTHEND UNITED, April 1909

This card shows Norwich City and Southend United players lining up for the kick-off of the Southern League clash on 22nd April 1909. A goal from City's England amateur international centre-forward Cyril Dunning and a second, in his own net, by United's goalie Charles Cotton, gave the 'Canaries' a 2−0 victory to keep them off the bottom of the table with just two fixtures of the season remaining (see also page 12). This card also offers a good view of the old Newmarket Road stand although two of the advertisement sections on the top have quite obviously been masked.

ROBERT HUGHES BEALE, c. 1909

Maidstone-born Bobby Beale joined City from Brighton in May 1908 and in four seasons made 111 appearances in the 'Canaries' goal. Following heroics in the 3—1 cup defeat of Sunderland in 1911 he was immortalised in song, "D'ye ken John Peel" being suitably reworded to commemorate his brilliant display. In May 1912 he was transferred to Manchester United where further quality performances earned him selection for the Football League v. Scottish League in 1913. After the war he moved back to Kent and had one season each with Gillingham and Maidstone before calling it a day. He died in Dymchurch in 1950, aged 64.

NORWICH CITY F.C., 1909/10

For overall results, 1909/10 was a poor season; 17th in the league and a 1st round cup exit. Other events featured the team using a motor-bus for an away fixture for the first time, suffering another drubbing at Swindon (1−7 this time), fielding only 10 men and drawing 0−0 at Southampton, and reduced to 8 men for a time during a 0−5 defeat at Brighton. Former favourites Percy "Putt" Gooch and Duncan Ronaldson (above, 3rd row back, 5th and 4th from right) returned and newcomers Billy Hampson (see page 18) and Sam Wolstenholme (see page 23) arrived. Both would go on to chalk up over 140 appearances in club colours.

WILLIAM HAMPSON, c. 1910

Lancastrian Billy Hampson came to Norwich from Bury via Rochdale. Although predominantly a full-back, perhaps his finest hour came when switched to centre-forward for the 1911 cup clash with Sunderland. Scoring two of the goals in the 3−1 victory he was carried off the pitch shoulder high by jubilant fans after the final whistle. Altogether Billy played 141 senior games for Norwich (10 goals) before leaving for Newcastle in 1914 where he remained until 1927, collecting an F.A. Cup winners' medal in 1924 aged almost 40. He later turned to management with Carlisle (signing a young Bill Shankly) and Leeds. He died in Congleton in 1966, aged 81.

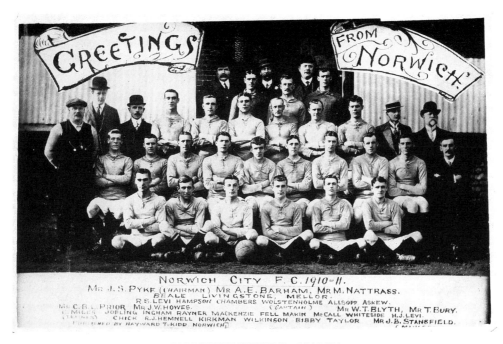

NORWICH CITY F.C. 1910-11.
Mr. J.S. PYKE (CHAIRMAN) Mr A.E. BARHAM, Mr M. NATTRASS.
BEALE LIVINGSTONE MELLOR.
R.S. LEVI HAMPSON CHAMBERS WOLSTENHOLME ALLSOPP ASKEW.
Mr C.B.L. PRIOR Mr J.W. HOWES. (CAPTAIN) Mr W.T. BLYTH, Mr T. BURY.
E. MILES JOBLING INGHAM RAYNER MACKENZIE FELL MAKIN McCALL WHITESIDE H.J. LEVI.
CHICK R.J. HEMNELL KIRKMAN WILKINSON BIBBY TAYLOR Mr J.B. STANSFIELD.
PUBLISHED BY HAYWARD T. KIDD NORWICH.

NORWICH CITY F.C., 1910/11

In addition to City's exciting cup win over first division Sunderland, the other main talking point of the season was the parading of the F.A. Cup at the Hospital Cup match on 10th September. Providing the opposition for the annual charity game, holders Newcastle United agreed to bring the cup with them to help swell the gate. As it happened, a record 13,473 people crammed into 'The Nest' (enlarged and improved during the close season) to watch the 1—1 draw and to catch a glimpse of the famous trophy. The 'Magpies' won the replay 3—0.

JOHN MACKENZIE, c. 1910

Scot 'Jock' MacKenzie followed manager James Stansfield from Carlisle to Norwich in May 1910. "A vigorous and fearless full-back" he missed only 5 first team matches in 5 seasons up to May 1915 and the intervention of war, and was first to reach 200 senior appearances for the club. Captain from 1913-14, his grand total of 204 included 91 consecutive games between 9th November 1911 and 10th January 1914. After the hostilities, during which he served as a lance-corporal with the R.G.A., he settled in the Midlands combining business with soccer in the Birmingham & District League. He is thought to have died in that area around 1940.

HAROLD JOSEPH LEVI, 1910

"H.J.", and his brother "R.S." (Reginald Samuel) were two of a dozen or so associated with both Norwich City and the ill-fated Croydon Common club before the first world war. Curiously though, whilst "H.J." made 22 first team appearances (2 goals) for City, he made none for the South Londoners. Conversely, "R.S." played twice for the 'Cock Robins' (1 goal) but never for the 'Canaries'. Others spending time at both clubs were Sam Bacon, Percy Barnfather, John Bowman (City's first professional manager), Billy Bushell, Herbert Chambers, Russell Hemnell, Will Jex, Walter Rayner, William Silor, George Thompson, Sam Wolstenholme and Ernest 'Tim' Williamson.

NORWICH CITY F.C. 1912-13.
BELL, HAMPSON, MELLOR, LONSDALE, SNAPE, WOODLANDS.
HARTLEY, WOLSTENHOLME, WOODS, HOUGHTON, PEARSON, POTTER.
MILES, INGHAM, SUTCLIFFE, BEEVERS, TRAVIS, HUGHES, CURTIN, BAUCHOP, MACKENZIE, J.B. STANSFIELD.
(TRAINER)   (SECRETARY)
HAYWARD KIDD, PUBLISHER, BANK PLAIN, NORWICH.

NORWICH CITY F.C., 1912/13

Another indifferent league campaign ended with City third from bottom, managing only 39 goals from 38 games, their all-time record low in the Southern League. Not for the first time, it was the F.A. Cup that provided most interest. Drawn away to second division Leicester Fosse (changed to Leicester City in 1919) in round 1, the match was played in a blizzard and was abandoned, goalless, after 65 minutes. Surprisingly, City won the replay 4−1 to set up an easier looking 2nd round tie with fellow Southern Leaguers Bristol Rovers (see also page 27) but after two drawn games they went out 0−1 in a second replay at neutral Stamford Bridge.

SAMUEL WOLSTENHOLME, c. 1912

Sam's route to Norwich took in Everton, Blackburn and Croydon Common. He arrived in April 1909 with three England caps v. Scotland (1904) plus Wales and Ireland (1905). He had also represented the Football League v. Scottish League and played twice for the North v. South. He gave sterling service to the 'Canaries', mostly at centre-half, and by the time he had moved on to Chester in 1913 he had made 145 appearances, scoring 8 goals. In June 1914, after injury had ended his playing days, he was appointed coach to the German F.A. but at the outbreak of war he was interned at Ruhleben. Whether or not he survived the ordeal is not known — can anyone confirm?

S. WOLSTENHOLME. HALF-BACK.
(CAPTAIN)
NORWICH CITY F.C.

NORWICH C. No. 7.

CROWD SCENE, EXETER, October 1912

Photographed at St. James' Park, Exeter during Norwich City's visit for the Southern League fixture on 19th October 1912. As was the custom in those days, everyone is seen wearing some form of head gear (see also page 6). The two ladies towards the front look splendid in their hats and seem quite content, perhaps anticipating the 1—0 home win that would eventually result. The goal was scored by inside-right Ellis Crompton, one of only six goals he scored in five seasons with the 'Grecians'. He died in Barnstaple in 1953, aged 66. Interestingly, the writer of the card claims he is in the picture but he doesn't say where. (Could he be the man with his hand up and smoking a pipe — centre right?).

WILLIAM INGHAM, c. 1912

Bury-born Billy Ingham was signed from another of James Stansfield's old clubs, Rossendale United, in May 1910. At 5'7" he was on the short side but his considerable skills more than made up for his lack of height. He was City's top scorer in 1910/11 with 15 goals from 40 starts and he went on to notch up 33 in 128 appearances before moving to Darlington in summer 1914. His ability was twice recognised in 1913 when he was selected to represent the Southern League against Scottish and Irish counterparts. He is believed to have died in Blackburn in 1955, aged 68.

W. INGHAM. FORWARD.
NORWICH CITY F.C.

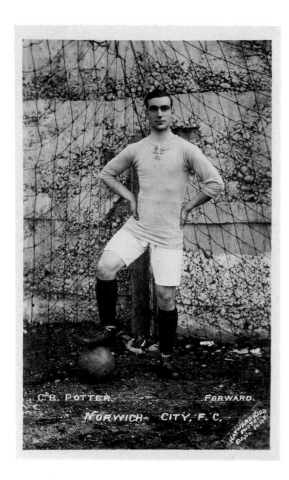

C.B. POTTER. FORWARD.
NORWICH CITY. F.C.

CECIL BERTRAM POTTER, c. 1912

Sussex-born Cecil Potter arrived from Ipswich Town, who were still an amateur side, in August 1911 and made an immediate impact, scoring 5 times in his first 8 outings. Equally at home on either wing or leading the attack he totalled 33 goals from 133 games up to the outbreak of the war. After the war he went into management and following spells in charge of Hartlepool, Derby and Huddersfield, he returned to Norwich late in 1926 to take over from James Stansfield. Unfortunately his success as a player wasn't repeated as manager (although he did sign the legendary Percy Varco) and shortly after the humiliating 0—5 home cup defeat by amateur club Corinthians in January 1929, he resigned. He died in Sutton, Surrey in 1975, aged 86.

NORWICH CITY v. BRISTOL ROVERS, February 1913

City skipper Sam Wolstenholme (centre) heads clear during the F.A. Cup 2nd round replay at 'The Nest' on 6th February 1913 (see also page 22). After 13,173 spectators packed into the ground the gates were closed. The match ended 2−2 after extra time with Harry Woods and Percy Sutcliffe netting City's goals. Other City players in shot are 'Jock' MacKenzie (2nd left), Will Bauchop (3rd left, in distance) and 'Jack' Houghton (right foreground, back to camera), who died in San Diego, California January 1991, 8 months short of his 100th birthday. Note the aforementioned concrete wall now appears complete − and the 'Spion Kop' terracing soaring high above.

'THE NEST', c. 1913

A close-up of the eastern end of the north stand and part of the massive 'Spion Kop'. It was most likely photographed during the City v. Bristol Rovers cup-tie of February 1913 (see page 27). Note the figures, including a police sergeant on the roof, and the unusual zig-zag arrangement of the 'Spion Kop' terracing with its varying levels and drops. It must have been quite an experience spectating from that section of the ground.

ARTHUR WOLSTENHOLME, 1913/14

Arthur had just one season at Norwich, but in that time he was not only top scorer with 15 goals from 36 games but he also became the only City player to bag 4 goals in a Southern League match — this coming in the 6—0 home win against Southend on 3rd January 1914. Although no relation to Sam Wolstenholme, like Sam, Arthur hailed from Lancashire and before joining City from Gillingham he had been with Oldham and Blackpool. After Norwich his travels took in Lincoln (1914), Oldham again (1919), Newport (1920), Darlington (1921) and Nelson (1922-24, where he latterly assisted the training staff). He died in Manchester in 1958, aged 67.

A.WOLSTENHOLME.   CENTRE FORWARD.
NORWICH CITY F.C.

NORWICH CITY v. WATFORD, 4th September 1913

This action photograph was taken at the Rosary Road (west) end of 'The Nest' and shows Arthur Wolstenholme (5th from right, partly hidden, facing goal) and others waiting to pounce as the ball is played into the Watford goalmouth from the right. Arthur didn't actually score in this season opener but goals from Billy Ingham, Harry Woods and an own goal from Watford's Charles Bulling secured City's 3–1 win. All this after Billy Hampson had put into his own net to present the 'Hornets' with a fourth minute lead. City then had to wait another 12 games before registering their next win. (See facing page for details).

NORWICH CITY v. WEST HAM UNITED, November 1913

Farnborough referee, Mr. W. Mortimer, and West Ham skipper, Tom Randall, join 'Jock' MacKenzie for the toss before the start of the Southern League match on 15th November 1913. Notwithstanding the sparsely populated appearance of the terraces, so near to kick-off, an estimated 7,000 spectators watched City record only their second win of the season — Billy Ingham's second half strike deciding the issue. It was one of only 9 victories gained the whole season, City's worst ever in the Southern League. 17 draws, however, helped them finish in 14th place and clear of danger.

A. WOODLANDS. HALF BACK
NORWICH CITY. F.C.

ARTHUR WOODLAND, c. 1913

As a junior, Arthur Woodland (not Woodlan<u>d</u>s as captioned) might have joined Everton, but he opted instead for St. Helens Town and it was from there City secured his signature in May 1912. Ever present during 1912/13, his 3 seasons' tally of 90 league/cup appearances and 2 goals would have been more had not injury sidelined him for all but 11 games in 1913/14. Joining the Royal Field Artillery in 1915, he still retained links with the club, returning occasionally whenever service in France and India permitted. In January 1920 he signed for Notts County and then had a season at Southend, ending June 1923. His demise is still being checked.

A NORWICH CITY XI, c. 1914

A City XI pose for the camera "just before the war". This suggests the date is sometime during 1914/15. If so it was the season City and first division Bradford City were ordered to play their F.A. Cup 3rd round 2nd replay behind closed doors at Sincil Bank, Lincoln, so as not to disrupt vital war work at a nearby munitions factory. However, when a crowd gathered outside the ground and tried to force entry, the gates were opened at half-time and around 1,000 saw City go down by 2 late goals to nil. Earlier they beat second division Nottingham Forest (away) 4−1 and first division Tottenham Hotspur (home) 3−2.

NORWICH CITY F.C., 1918/19

The City team photographed with the Norwich Hospital Cup which they retained by beating Boulton & Paul at 'The Nest' on 17th May 1919. The works XI had several former and future 'Canaries' in their line-up and both teams saw the match as an opportunity to prove a point. In an ill-tempered encounter, B. & P's 'Pompey' Martin and Bill Barclay, along with City's Jack Doran (seated above, holding ball), were sent off after an 'unsavoury incident'. It seems the only charity in evidence was the £53 donated to the Hospital Fund from gate receipts. Doran and Sam Jennings (on Doran's left) scored for City, 'Tricky' Hawes (penalty) replied for B. & P.

NORWICH CITY SQUAD, 1919/20

In this their last season in the Southern League, City had Major Frank Buckley (above, back, 2nd from right) as player/manager in his first managerial post. Under him they finished 12th in the table and were unceremoniously dumped out of the cup at the first hurdle, 0−5 at Darlington. In 43 games a staggering 40 different players were used − a club record that still stands − although several were virtual one match trialists. Major Buckley, with only one appearance in City colours himself, left in June 1920 and, in turn, managed Blackpool, Wolves (17 years), Notts County, Hull, Leeds and Walsall with distinction, retiring June 1955. He died in Walsall, December 1964, aged 81.

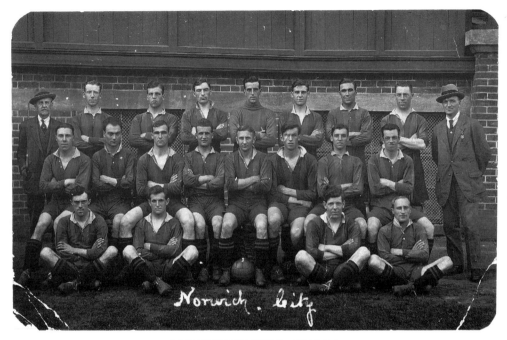

NORWICH CITY F.C., 1920/21

At the beginning of the 1920/21 season, Norwich City and 20 other Southern League clubs formed the Football League's new Third Division. Any thoughts City harboured that the change would improve their fortunes soon evaporated as they struggled for points just as before. Only 7 came from the first 13 games and the season was exactly a third of the way through (match 14) before any victory gained. At the end of the season their final position was 16th with 36 points. Coincidentally, City's opening match was held at Plymouth; the same venue as their Southern League debut in 1905/06. It produced their first goal, Vic Whitham (middle row, 4th from left) scoring, and first point in a 1−1 draw.

NORWICH CITY v. LUTON TOWN, August 1921

Saturday, 27th August 1921 and the City team take to the field for their opening fixture of the new season against Luton Town. Judging by the strong shadows it was a glorious day with the ground, and expectant 11,000 crowd, bathed in sunshine. What a pity then the result didn't match the weather — a solitary second-half goal by Irish International Allan Mathieson winning both points for the 'Hatters'. One of the best general views of 'The Nest' found on a postcard. It provides an excellent panorama of the St. Leonard's Road end and shows the full extent of the wall and the height of the 'Spion Kop'.

CHARLES MILES, p.u. 5th October, 1920

After his appointment as City Manager in 1905, John Bowman's first task was to appoint Kentishman Charlie Miles as team trainer. This accomplished gymnast spent 3 years as Gymnastics Instructor at Tunbridge Wells Grammar School before joining New Brompton F.C. (renamed Gillingham, 1911) as trainer in 1899. 3 years later he moved to Q.P.R. where his skill, dedication and enthusiasm greatly impressed Bowman. 'Milo', affectionately dubbed "the man who touches the spot", ranked with the best trainers in the country. After the 1914−18 war he had 2 seasons with South Shields but returned to Norwich in 1922/23 and remained until retiring in 1927. Staying on in Norfolk he died in Hainford in June 1946, aged 78.

HERBERT EDWARD SKERMER, 1921

One of a long line of fine City 'custodians' down the years, Nottinghamshire-born Herbert Skermer was snapped up from Hartsey Colliery by Major Frank Buckley in December 1919. He played in 22 of the last 25 Southern League games of 1919/20 and became City's first Football League keeper in 1920/21, throughout which he was ever present. After 95 appearances in the 'Canaries' goal, Herbert surprisingly reverted to non-league football firstly with Coalville Swifts in November 1922 and then Loughborough Corinthians in 1924/25. In 1934, he returned to Norwich and managed the Lame Dog public house in Queen's Road until his untimely death, aged 58, in November 1954.

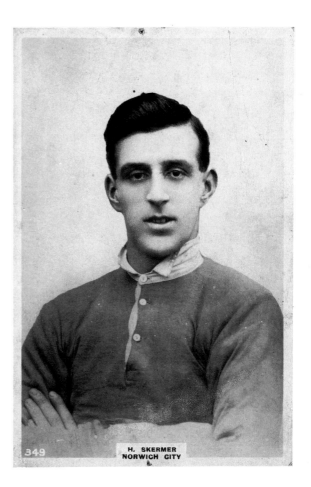

H. SKERMER
NORWICH CITY

349

BENJAMIN GEORGE SMITH, c. 1921

Norwich born left-back 'Benny' Smith's association with City began in September 1916 and ended abruptly eight and a half years later. A regular guest player throughout the war he signed amateur forms in April 1919 and totted up 110 senior appearances (no goals) by the time an F.A. Commission adjudged him guilty of 'coupon betting'; suspended him 'sine die' in January 1924. "A fearless, keen tackler and great trier", Benny was one of 12 players to represent City in both Southern and Football Leagues. He also served C.E.Y.M.S. and Boulton & Paul and gained Norfolk County honours. He died in Norwich in July 1972, almost 80.

ISAAC GEORGE MARTIN, 1921

Considering Gateshead-born George Martin played only a handful of games for Portsmouth prior to joining Norwich in July 1913, 'Pompey' was a surprising nickname for the former Sunderland stopper. However, it was the one that stuck with him throughout a colourful 'Canary' career that spanned 14 seasons and earned 2 testimonials. His wholehearted displays at the centre of City's defence made him a great favourite as he amassed 337 appearances, 207 as captain. His solitary goal came in the 6−3 defeat of Bournemouth played on the 9th October, 1924. After retiring in 1927 this silver haired character remained a regular sight around town for many years until his death in May 1962, aged 72.

484

G. MARTIN
NORWICH CITY

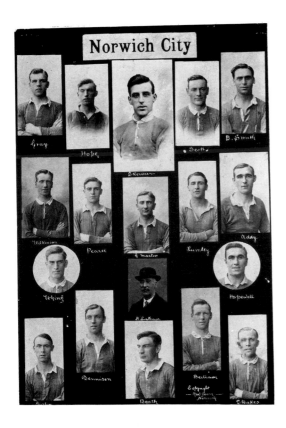

Norwich City

Gray, Hope, S Keemer, Scott, B Smith, Wilkinson, Pearce, F Martin, Lumley, Addy, Utting, Hopewell, A Latham, Austin, Dennison, Booth, Betham, S Stakes

NORWICH CITY SQUAD, 1921/22

The 1921/22 squad, featured here individually, could finish no higher than 15th in the league — their new yellow and green striped shirts obviously failing to inspire. The cup brought some solace with wins over the intriguing Metrogas (played in the Old Kent Road, London) and Oxford City but further progress was halted by Barnsley in a first round proper replay. At 'The Nest' on Easter Monday 1922, part of the fencing on top of the retaining wall gave way, resulting in 60 people falling to the ground some way below. Miraculously, only one small boy with a cut head needed prolonged treatment and the game against Northampton proceeded as scheduled, City winning 2−0.

JAMES HENRY HANNAH, 1922

'Joe' joined Norwich as an amateur in 1920, from his home town club Sheringham, turning professional in June 1921. Equally adept at centre-forward, half-back or full-back, he gained his county cap in 1920/21. In 1925 he represented South v. North, Rest v. England and toured Australia with a F.A. party. Over 15 seasons, this fine all-rounder made 427 appearances (21 goals) for City, a club record surpassed only by Ashman, Stringer and Keelan, and earning his testimonial in 1932. He later coached Bury Town and in 1946 became steward at Sheringham's Morley Club until retiring to London in 1959. He died in Stepney in February 1975, aged 76.

NORWICH CITY SQUAD, 1924/25

Players and officials assemble before the start of the 1924/25 campaign — note the all-white shirts introduced the previous year. Another disappointing season produced only a few highlights. On Boxing Day, City thrashed Q.P.R. 5—0 at 'The Nest' but then lost by the same score at Plymouth the following day. In the F.A. Cup they foundered 0—4 at Notts County in round 2, finishing with only nine men, but then blasted West Ham 6—1 to win the Hospital Cup for the first time against Football League opposition. Frank McCudden (back row, third player from right) and Jimmy Jackson (middle row, third player from left) each scored three goals.

ISAAC TERENCE RYDER, 1925

Terry Ryder made only three league appearances for City, all at centre-forward, and finished on the losing side each time. Norwich-born, he came from local amateurs City Wanderers in January 1924 but was always in competition with the more experienced McCudden, Jackson and Ernie North. Even so his average of a goal every 2 games for the reserves suggests a potential that was, perhaps, never fully tested. Released in 1926 he returned to local football with C.E.Y.M.S. 20 years later his son, Terence Roy Ryder, made his 'Canary' debut to create a father/son first for the club. Terry junior (1946–50) made 51 appearances and scored 12 goals.

JOSEPH JOBLING, 1927/28

The front of this card features Gorleston F.C. but it is the back, presumably written by a disgruntled official, that is interesting from a Norwich City point of view. The Geordie-born half-back joined Norwich from Gorleston in August 1928 and played 75 times (1 goal) before leaving for Charlton in March 1932. He remained at 'The Valley' until 1947 — guesting for several other clubs, including Norwich, during the war — and gained a War Cup winners medal against Chelsea in 1944. Returning to Norfolk, Joe rejoined the 'Greens' as committee member then manager and retained links with Charlton until his death in July 1969, shortly before his 63rd birthday.

A SEASIDE STROLL, November 1927

City players pictured along Gorleston's Lower Esplanade a few days before their F.A. Cup first round clash with Poole Town on 26th November 1927: a seaside stroll was always an integral part of City's cup-tie preparations. Les Robinson netted to earn a 1−1 draw in Dorset then a Percy Varco hat-trick and goal each from Robinson and Alf Moule won the replay 5−0. In round 2, City travelled to Luton and crashed 0−6; their heaviest ever F.A. Cup defeat. From left to right, the above players are: Slicer, Lamb, Campbell, Robinson, McGrae, Moule, Porter, Varco, Pembleton, Richmond, Dennington, Hannah and Young (trainer).

NORWICH CITY XI, 1928/29

This City team drew 3—3 (Porter 2, Varco) at Walsall in the league on 15th December 1928. *Back,* left to right: Lamb, Young (trainer), Hannah, Dennington, Richmond, Potter (manager), McGrae. *Front:* Porter, Stephenson, Varco, McKenna, Slicer, Greenwell. "Give it to Varco" was the cry in those days as the popular Cornishman bagged 32 goals, a new club record, in 1927/28. He looked set fair for many more but added only 15 to that total as injury limited his subsequent appearances to just 21 — and prompted his departure for Exeter in February 1930. In 1928/29 City finished seventeenth in the table and lost heavily to Corinthians in the cup (see page 26).

NORWICH CITY F.C., 1929/30

This was City's best season yet in the Football League. A final position of eighth might have been fourth had they not lost their last 3 games, 2 of them at home. Their 88 goals — another record — were aided by the record 10−2 victory over Coventry City on 15th March 1930. Five of the goals came from Tommy Hunt (front row, right of centre) who finished the season top scorer with 25. Another 10−2 statistic resulted from the 2 matches against Merthyr Town — City winning both 5−1. In the cup, City lost in round 1, ironically at Coventry, 0−2 after a 3−3 draw in Norwich.

Jobling, Hannah, Lochhead, Scott, Crompton, Wharton, Brain, Wallbanks, Wren, Thompson, Robinson,
Young, Hunt, Burditt, Smith, Jordan, Ogle, Williamson, Williams, Murphy, Blakemore, Hawes,
(Trainer) (Asst. Trainer)
McGregor, Taylor, Brown, Pearson, Bell, Slack, Hall.

NORWICH CITY FOOTBALL TEAM. 1931—1932.

NORWICH CITY F.C., 1931/32

In contrast to 1929/30 (page 49), 1930/31 was a total disaster as, for the first time, the 'Canaries' finished bottom of the table on goal average. Comfortably re-elected, 1931/32 was far better — 10th place being more respectable than spectacular, although there were some notable scorelines like 7—0 against Thames, 6—0 against Bristol Rovers, 6—2 against Coventry, all at home and 1—7 against Luton away. Percy Varco scored twice against his old club when City lost 0—3 at Exeter on 2nd April 1932 — the date also marking the 'Canary' debut of Bernard Robinson (see page 53). In the cup: a 3—1 win at Wimbledon was followed by a 1—4 defeat at Brentford.

NORWICH CITY F.C., 1933/34

Having finished a splendid third in 1932/33, City commenced 1933/34 with a flying start, taking 9 points out of 10 to lead the table. They remained top of the table 28 weeks out of 34 and were headed only once after 4th November. An unbeaten run of 16 games from 6th January to 7th April, with just one defeat in the last 20, kept them on course for their first promotion which they clinched on the 21st April following a 3—1 win over second-placed Coventry. Their five away defeats was the lowest in all four divisions and only Second Division champions Grimsby with 26 gained more away points than City's 25.

THIRD DIVISION (SOUTH) CHAMPIONSHIP PRESENTATION, 5th May 1934

Skipper Stan Ramsay congratulated by Everton F.C. chairman, Mr. W. C. Cuff, as he steps forward to receive the Division Three (South) championship shield after the final match of 1933/34 against Bristol Rovers (h), 0—0. On Ramsay's right, wearing spectacles, is City's vice-chairman and former player George Pilch, and behind are team mates Tommy Halliday, Jack Vinall and Norman Wharton. Chairman Billy Hurrell is on the far left holding the trophy. The following Monday evening, 7th May, at 'The Nest' the team celebrated their success in grand style by crushing Division Two champions Grimsby Town 7—2 in the Hospital Cup. Vinall netted 5, Alf Kirchen 2.

BERNARD CECIL ROBINSON, c. 1934

Cambridge-born wing-half 'Barney' Robinson joined City from King's Lynn in December 1931 and made 380 league/cup appearances (14 goals). But for the war, during which he played around 160 'other' games, his total would have been nearer 600. A long throw-in specialist with an unusual penalty taking technique, he rarely suffered loss of form and his eighteen years loyal service were rewarded with a testimonial in 1949. When he retired from football, he became the landlord at the Ipswich Tavern in central Norwich. 'Barney' is now retired, living with his wife at Sprowston where they both enjoy a game of golf.

NORWICH CITY v. ARSENAL, May 1935

6th May 1935 is remembered as the date of the Silver Jubilee of King George V and Queen Mary, but for Norwich City the date has an added significance, marking their last appearance at 'The Nest' (see page 55). The occasion was the Hospital Cup match and their opponents Arsenal, with former City winger Alf Kirchen in their side, won 1—0. Here the 'Canaries' and the 'Gunners' pose with officials before the match. Kirchen (see page 61) is seated, 2nd left, 2nd row back. After the game the players of both teams remained on the pitch to listen, with the 15,550 capacity crowd, to His Majesty's Jubilee wireless broadcast relayed around the ground.

CARROW ROAD, Summer 1935

On 15th May 1935, the F.A. informed Norwich City that 'The Nest', their quaint little home for 27 years, was inadequate for the demands of second division football. Responding quickly, the Board considered several options, but decided on new premises in Carrow Road; headquarters of Boulton & Paul's Sports Club. Work commenced at 3.45 <u>a.m.</u> on 11th June and by 31st August, astonishingly just 82 days later, the site had been transformed into a modern stadium ready for the new season. Delighted City officials declared it the '8th Wonder of the World'. This picture was taken from the River Wensum end looking north-east, and shows the grandstand under construction.

CARROW ROAD OPENING CEREMONY, 31st August 1935

Supported by "a company of representatives from the city and county", Mr. Russell Colman, Lord Lieutenant of Norwich and newly appointed club president, unties the yellow and green silk ribbons across the entrance to the pitch to officially open the Carrow Road ground. Amongst the guests from the football world was Jimmy 'Punch' McEwen, City's skipper in 1905/06 (see page 4) who attended on behalf of Arsenal F.C. The Second Division match v. West Ham immediately followed and 29,779 spectators roared City on to a thrilling 4—3 victory. The ground's first ever goal came from City captain Doug Lochhead after 10 minutes. Jack Vinall (2) and Billy Warnes added the others.

KIMBOLTON SCHOOL v. NORWICH CITY, November 1935

Players and officials of Kimbolton School and Norwich City face the camera before the annual charity match at Kimbolton on 6th November 1935. The School XI − reinforced with 'Canaries' Jack Scott (standing, 6th left), Les Maskell (seated, 4th right) and manager Tom Parker (seated, 5th left) − were easily beaten 5−1 by a mainly reserve strength City team captained by Old Kimboltonian goalkeeper, J. G. Dixon (seated, 5th right). The match, refereed by renowned Spurs and England winger and Test Match umpire, 'Fanny' Walden (standing, 2nd left), raised £25 for Huntingdon County Hospital. Glyn Davies and George Ansell, City players in the 1930s, both taught at Kimbolton where, also, Parker coached soccer.

NORWICH CITY SQUAD WITH TEAM 'BUS, c. 1936

The entire City squad muster in Carrow Road in front of the team 'bus — a 1935, scarlet and cream, 32-seater, Bristol J.JW coach owned by the Eastern Counties Omnibus Company. Photographed looking east with Boulton & Paul's Joinery Works on the left. Eighth right is Glaswegian Doug Lochhead who between June 1929 and March 1950 served City as player (222 appearances, 5 goals), captain, scout and assistant, caretaker and full-time manager. He died in Leeds in 1968. Ninth left, in black, is Jack Vinall whose 80 goals from 181 games (August 1933 — September 1937) ranks him as one of the club's most successful strikers; he now lives in Worcester.

NORWICH CITY F.C., 1936/37

In this their third season in Division 2, City had fine wins at Tottenham, Newcastle and Blackpool (eventual runners-up), thrashed Aston Villa (h) 5−1 and 'doubled' Nottingham Forest, scoring 4 times in each game, but overall their league performance was disappointing − slipping to 17th in the table from 14th in 1934/35 and 11th in 1935/36. Against First Division opposition in the cup they beat Liverpool (h) 3−1; Jack Vinall scoring twice in the opening 5 minutes. City then held Bolton (a) 1−1 before going down 1−2 after extra time in the replay. Twelve days later manager Tom Parker (seated second row, extreme right) left to join Southampton, his home club.

ROYAL VISIT, October 1938

It was a real red-letter day for Norwich City on Saturday 29th October 1938 when King George VI, on a tour of the city, visited Carrow Road and watched the first 15 minutes of the Division Two match against Millwall. It was the first time a Second Division game had been attended by a reigning monarch. The occasion, however, proved too much for the 'Canaries' as they went down 0—2. The score was 0—0 when His Majesty departed from the ground. In this picture the King arrives inside the ground accompanied on his left by the new City chairman, James Wright. Note the young lad, right of flag, who forgot to come to attention.

ALFRED JOHN KIRCHEN, c. 1938

Alf had made just 18 senior appearances (10 goals) when Arsenal paid City £6,000 for his services in March 1935. The speedy, free-scoring winger from Shouldham then hit 88 goals in 162 games for the 'Gunners' by the outbreak of war, gaining championship and cup winners medals and 3 England caps, along the way. Damaged knee ligaments ended his sparkling career in September 1943, precipitating his return to Norfolk where he coached the 'Canaries' for a time and then appointed a club director until 1957. Now retired, the award-winning farmer — and former clay pigeon champion — still lives locally and, approaching 80, remains fit and active playing bowls.

KIRCHEN

NORWICH CITY FOOTBALL CLUB LIMITED

Telephone :
NORWICH 21514

CARROW ROAD
NORWICH

10/9/45

Dear Dick,
Can you manage Gillingham on Saturday? Bus leaves Carrow Road at 8-30 am. Let me know by return if you can make it. Kind regards
Yours Sincerely
D. Lochhead.

CLUB POSTCARD, September 1945

This is one of Norwich City's own postcards used at a time when telephone contact was not as commonplace as it is today. In this instance manager Doug Lochhead is notifying Richard Sparkes, a Beccles United amateur who assisted the 'Canaries' during the 1945/46 'Transitional' season, of the game at Gillingham on 15th September. Dick did 'make' it and played right-back in a match billed as a 'return friendly'. The result was a 3—3 draw and all of City's goals were scored by Robin Newsome; a guest from West Bromwich Albion. The card incidentally is white with green printing. The telephone number, of course, has since been changed.

NORWICH CITY F.C., 1948/49

Having been relegated in 1938/39, City started the post-war era back in Division 3 (South) and struggled badly. Second from bottom in each of the first two seasons meant they twice had to seek re-election. It seemed 1948/49 would follow the same pattern as three defeats resulted from the first four games, but a 4—0 home win against Bristol City steadied the boat and, although form fluctuated, they slowly climbed to safety, finishing 10th — and won the return at Ashton Gate 6—1. The Wembley trail ended tamely at Torquay after a home victory against Wellington Town (now Telford United). Terry Ryder junior (see page 45) is seated, right foreground.

NORWICH CITY FOOTBALL CLUB 1950-51

J. Macdonald, E. Arnold, J. Duffy, R. Ashman, J. Summers, L. Owens, W. Atkinson, I. Armes, B. Jones,
H. Proctor (*Trainer*), J. Gavin, R. Hollis, R. Foulkes, D. Edwards, G. Ephgrave, K. Nethercott, B. Holmes,
M. Tobin, T. Docherty, W. Furness (*Trainer*),
P. Gordon, W. Lewis, L. Eyre, C. Birch, N. Low (*Manager*), J. L. Hanly (*Chairman*), P. Dash (*Secretary*), T. Ryder,
L. Dutton, D. Morgan, J. Evans
N. Kinsey   D. Pickwick

NORWICH CITY F.C., 1950/51

A club record twenty-three games without defeat kept City in promotion contention for most of the season but with only one to go up they took just four points out of the final ten and had to settle for runners-up spot; six points behind champions Nottingham Forest. The cup campaign began quietly with wins over Watford (h) and Rhyl (a) but then exploded into life when Liverpool were again conquered, 3−1 at Carrow Road, to complete an amazing hat-trick of City cup wins over the Anfield men. A 2−0 victory at Newport then set up a 5th round trip to Sunderland but in front of a massive 65,125 crowd, City bowed out 1−3.

RONALD GEORGE ASHMAN, c. 1950

Ron arrived from Whittlesey, Cambridgeshire, in May 1944 and when he and club parted company in June 1966 he had amassed 662 appearances, scored 56 goals and developed from a raw, often barracked, young centre-forward into a polished half/full-back, inspirational captain, fine coach and astute manager. His all-round contribution to Norwich City's cause was immense, his achievements too many to list. For certain the former 'Bevin Boy' was one of the greatest 'Canaries' of all time. Ron later had spells managing Scunthorpe (twice) — transferring Keegan and Clemence to Liverpool — and Grimsby, retiring in 1981 to become a partner in a Scunthorpe Travel Agency — a position he still holds today.

JOHN THOMAS GAVIN, c. 1950

Originally signed from Limerick in August 1948, Johnny netted 79 times in 221 games before being lured to Tottenham in October 1954. When he returned 13 months later as part of the deal which took Maurice Norman to White Hart Lane, a further 53 goals from 117 appearances made his aggregate 132 goals/338 games and established a club record that may now never be broken. In summer 1958 the 7 times capped Republic of Ireland winger was released and he joined Watford then Crystal Palace, Cambridge City and Newmarket Town. A latter day publican and painter/decorator, Johnny lives in Cambridge and recently underwent hip replacement surgery.

KENNETH WALTER SAMUEL NETHERCOTT,
c. 1950

Ken, a former Bristol City amateur, joined Norwich in April 1947 and became one of the best keepers outside the First Division, gaining England 'B' honours and attracting the attentions of Arsenal. After a bad knock in December 1953 he lost confidence and spent 4 seasons in and out of the first team, sharing duties with Ken Oxford. When Oxford moved to Derby in December 1957 Nethercott resumed as unrivalled number one but in February 1959 he dislocated his right shoulder and that effectively ended his career. Released in June 1960, after 416 games, he had one season at Wisbech before calling it a day. Still lives in Norwich.

NORWICH CITY SQUAD, January 1952

City players answering a photo-call at Carrow Road a few hours before their 3rd round F.A. Cup clash with Arsenal on 12th January 1952. Those pictured are: *back row,* left to right: Low (Manager), Gavin, Lewis, Hollis, Foulkes, Nethercott, Ashman, Ackerman, Proctor (Trainer). *Front row:* Jones, Rackham, Morgan, Kinsey, Dutton. From the 12 players selected Gavin was omitted in favour of the less experienced Denys Jones. The ploy failed to trouble the 'Gunners' though as they ran out easy 5−0 victors with goals from Doug Lishman (2), Peter Goring, Don Roper and Jimmy Logie. They went on to reach the final but were beaten 0−1 by Newcastle.

NORWICH CITY v. ARSENAL, January 1952

City goalie Ken Nethercott makes a good save to thwart an Arsenal attack whilst Ashman (6), Morgan, Dutton, Foulkes (5) and Lewis (3) and Arsenal's Lishman, Goring (9) and Cox (7) look on. Nethercott's goal was under threat for much of this 3rd round F.A. Cup-tie and he was forced into making several important stops as City's overworked defence desperately tried to contain the lively visiting attack. It was perhaps this fine performance that provoked the 'Gunners' interest in the City keeper (see page 67). Watched by a near capacity crowd of 38,964 the match produced gate receipts of £5,482.11s; a record for Norwich at the time.

DUTCH TOUR PARTY, May 1952

The City party pose outside Thorpe Station on Saturday, 17th May 1952 before embarking on the club's first overseas trip — a 12-day, 4-match tour of Holland — during which the team beat Enschede Combined XI (1—0), Hague Combined XI (2—1), Sittardia (3—0) and Haarlem Combined XI (3—1). Left to right: Low (manager), Duffy, Coxon, Foulkes, Morgan, Dash (secretary), Furness (trainer), Lewis, Kinsey, Hollis, Pickwick, Ashman, Dutton, Jones, McCrohan, Summers, Nethercott, Proctor (trainer), Gavin. These 19 were joined by Messrs. Hanly (chairman), Hurn (vice-chairman) and Murphy (club doctor). The tour livery comprised green blazer with club badge, grey flannel trousers, white shirt, yellow/green striped tie, black shoes.

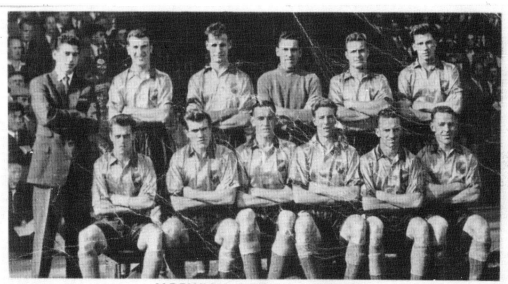

NORWICH CITY F.C. — 1956-57
BACK ROW *(l. to r.)* **Chung : McCrohan : Englefield : Oxford : Lockwood : Pointer**
FRONT ROW *(l. to r.)* **Bacon : Gordon : McNeil** *(Capt.)* **: Hunt : Gavin : Kitchener**

NORWICH CITY XI, 1956/57

In a season fraught with problems the club found itself in dire financial straits and had to rely on an Appeal Fund to keep going. The team slumped to bottom of the table during a run of 26 consecutive games without a win (which saw them also lose at home to non-league Bedford Town in the cup) and, for the 4th time in history, had to seek re-election. On the plus side: Carrow Road's new floodlights were inaugurated in October 1956 and Ralph Hunt scored another 20 goals to add to the 31 bagged in 1955/56. He would eventually reach 72 in 132 games; a strike rate better than Gavin's.

NORFOLK CAMERA CENTRE.

R. McCROHAN   B. THURLOW   K. NETHERCOTT   B. BUTLER   R. ASHMAN   M. CROWE

E. CROSSAN   T. ALLCOCK   T. BLY   J. HILL   B. BRENNAN

NORWICH CITY 'CUP' XI, 1958/59

The above eleven, with 'Sandy' Kennon later replacing the injured Nethercott (see page 67), won wide acclaim by reaching the F.A. Cup semi-finals and so nearly becoming the first Third Division side to reach the final. They beat Ilford, Swindon, Manchester United, Cardiff, Tottenham and Sheffield United only to fail at the last hurdle against Luton; the Wembley dream ending in a replay at St. Andrews where Billy Bingham's decider put the 'Hatters' through to meet Nottingham Forest. In the league, City finished 4th, missing promotion by four points. Twelve months later, as runners-up to Southampton, they returned to Division 2 after an absence of 21 years. (See also front cover).

ROBERT ANDERSON BRENNAN, c. 1959

Belfast-born Bobby Brennan arrived at Norwich from Fulham in July 1953 for a then record £15,000 having previously played for Distillery, Luton and Birmingham. He ranked amongst the best inside forwards of his day, winning 5 Northern Ireland caps, and was certainly one of the most skilful players ever to don the 'Canary' shirt. Prematurely released in August 1956, he joined Yarmouth Town but was brought back by Archie Macaulay in March 1957 and, converted to left wing, he starred in City's 1958/59 cup run. Released again in 1960 after 250 appearances and 52 goals, he briefly coached King's Lynn. Now 67 the former car salesman lives in Sprowston.

NORWICH CITY F.C., 1961/62

A season of struggle rescued by cup activity. In the F.A. Cup, City reached round 5, going out 1−3 at Sheffield United, after two classic encounters with neighbours Ipswich Town in round 4. A 1−1 draw at home was followed by a 2−1 victory at Portman Road − Terry Allcock (4th left, 2nd row) scoring all three City goals. In the League Cup, inaugurated the previous season, wins against Chesterfield, Lincoln, Middlesborough, Sunderland and Blackpool put the 'Canaries' into the two-legged final against Rochdale, which they won 4−0 on aggregate to lift their first ever national knock-out trophy. In Division Two they finished 17th, 6 points clear of relegation.

CARROW ROAD, 1962

This aerial view of Carrow Road was taken approaching from the north-west on an unidentified matchday. Note three sides of the ground are now under cover. In 1937 the 'Thorpe' or 'Railway' end terracing was roofed over and named the Barclay Stand after benefactor and vice-president, Capt. Evelyn Barclay. The centre section of the South Stand was erected during summer 1959, extended to the 'River' end a year later and linked up with the 'Barclay' at the end of 1961/62. The whole project cost around £80,000 and was funded entirely by the Supporters' Club. This picture was also the centre piece of the club's official 1962 Christmas card.

JOSPEH MULLETT, February 1966

Born Small Heath, Joe's professional career began with nearby Birmingham City in 1955 but in 4 seasons he had just 3 league outings. Joining Norwich in February 1959 he found opportunities equally rare and played only 5 more games during his first 3 seasons there. His chance finally came in January 1962 when, replacing Matt Crowe at left-half and later switching to left-back, he established himself as a key defender and went on to register 246 appearances. His 5 goals included 3 penalties. 'Freed' in summer 1968 he spent 2 years at King's Lynn before returning to the Midlands to take over the Holly Bush public house in Cradley Heath.

NORWICH CITY SQUAD, 1971/72

'City's great leap year' saw the unfancied 'Canaries' achieve Division One status for the first time — and go up as champions. They led the table from match seven, were unbeaten after thirteen games and lost only once in their first twenty-one games. They faltered slightly at the turn of the year, going six games without a win, but stayed well on course for promotion which they clinched at Orient in the penultimate game of the season. The title was secured five days later at relegated Watford. They went out of both cups at home: 0−1 to Chelsea (League Cup, round 5) and 0−3 to Hull (F.A. Cup, round 3). *Back row,* left to right: Butler, Briggs, Anderson, Howard, Black. *Centre row:* Stringer, Forbes, Cawston, Keelan, Govier, Payne. *Seated:* Foggo, Paddon, Bennett, Livermore, Silvester.

NORWICH CITY SQUAD, 1974/75

In 1974/75, after two seasons in Division One, City were relegated to Division Two with Southampton and Manchester United but climbed back at the first attempt in third place behind United and Aston Villa. The 'Villans', managed by former City boss Ron Saunders, also inflicted City's second Wembley defeat on them, winning the League Cup final 1—0; Machin's spectacular handball, Keelan's fine penalty save and Graydon's winner from the rebound summing up a disappointing match. Villa then came to Carrow Road for the last game of the season and won 4—1 to really rub salt in City's wound. In the F.A. Cup, third round, City lost 0—2 at Coventry.

KEVIN DAMIEN KEELAN, c. 1979

Calcutta-born Kevin joined Norwich in July 1963 and on bidding farewell in February 1980, aged 39, had appeared 681 times in City's goal to top their all-time list ironically one place ahead of Ron Ashman, the man who brought him from Wrexham. Flambuoyant, acrobatic and occasionally rash, he matured under Ron Saunders' influence into one of the most reliable, respected and popular keepers in the land and was unlucky never to gain representative honours. An M.B.E., awarded in June 1980, was a fitting consolation and tribute. Spells with New England Teamen and Tampa Bay Rowdies cultivated his liking for America so-much-so he has now made Florida his home.

CARROW ROAD, 1991

This recent aerial view of Carrow Road is again taken approaching from the north. After 1962 (see page 75) the much maligned seats were added to the South Stand at the end of 1974/75 and the River End complex was built in 1979 with the £1¼ million cost being aided by a supporters' Building Bond scheme. The new Grandstand, replacing the original wooden structure destroyed by fire in October 1984, was officially opened by H.R.H. The Duchess of Kent on St. Valentine's Day 1987 and the popular Barclay Stand was demolished during summer 1992 to make way for an all-seater replacement.